Spaghetti Cookbook

By Brad Hoskinson

Copyright 2023 by Brad Hoskinson. All rights reserved.

No part of this book may be reproduced in any form or by any electronic or mechanical means, including information storage and retrieval systems, without written permission from the author, except for the use of brief quotations in a book review.

Table of Contents

Favorite Baked Spaghetti 5

Broccoli Beef Lo Mein 7

Spaghetti Pork Chops 8

Pesto Shrimp Pasta 9

Ground Beef Spaghetti Skillet 10

My Best Spaghetti & Meatballs 11

Monterey Spaghetti 13

Spaghetti with Bacon 14

Stovetop Turkey Tetrazzini 15

Shrimp Puttanesca 16

Grandma's Cajun Chicken & Spaghetti 18

Florentine Spaghetti Bake 20

Spaghetti with Fresh Tomato Sauce 22

Spaghetti with Sausage and Peppers 23

Creamy Chicken Fettuccine 24

Pizza Spaghetti 25

Rustic Summer Vegetable Pasta 26

North Carolina Shrimp Saute 28

Grecian Pasta & Chicken Skillet 29

Quick Carbonara 31

Church Supper Spaghetti 32

Nana's Italian Roulade 33

Bruschetta-Topped Chicken & Spaghetti 35

Stamp-of-Approval Spaghetti Sauce 36

Mozzarella Baked Spaghetti 38

Rosemary Shrimp with Spaghetti 39

One-Pot Spaghetti Dinner 40

Southwestern Spaghetti 41
Slow-Cooker Spaghetti & Meatballs 42
Mushroom Turkey Tetrazzini 44

Favorite Baked Spaghetti

For those searching for a delicious and classic Italian dish, baked spaghetti is sure to be a hit. This well-loved favorite combines traditional Italian cuisine's flavors into one easy-to-make meal. From the tangy tomatoes to the savory seasonings, this dish is sure to tantalize your taste buds. Not only is it a delightful meal, but baked spaghetti is also incredibly easy to make.

TOTAL TIME: Prep: 30 min. Bake: 1 hour + standing

Ingredients

- 1.5 packages spaghetti
- 1.5 pounds of ground beef
- 2 medium onions, chopped
- 1.5 jars of pasta sauce
- 2/3 teaspoon seasoned salt
- 3 large eggs
- 2/3 cup grated Parmesan cheese
- 6 tablespoons butter, melted
- 2.5 cups 4% cottage cheese
- 5 cups shredded part-skim mozzarella cheese
- Chopped fresh basil, optional

Directions

1. Preheat oven to 370°. Cook spaghetti according to package directions for al dente. Meanwhile, in a large skillet, cook beef and onion over medium heat until beef is no longer pink and onion is tender, 9 minutes, breaking beef into crumbles; drain. Stir in pasta sauce and seasoned salt; set aside.
2. Whisk the eggs, Parmesan cheese, and butter in a large bowl. Drain spaghetti; add to egg mixture and toss to coat.
3. Place half the spaghetti mixture in a greased 13x9-in. or 3-qt. baking dish. Top with half the cottage cheese, meat sauce, and mozzarella cheese. Repeat layers. Place the baking dish on a rimmed baking sheet.

4. Cover and bake for 45 minutes. Uncover; bake until heated through, 30 minutes longer. Let stand 20 minutes before serving. If desired, sprinkle with basil.

Broccoli Beef Lo Mein

Broccoli Beef Lo Mein is a classic Chinese dish that has been enjoyed for generations. It combines the flavors of tender beef, fresh broccoli, and savory noodles to create a delicious and satisfying meal. This traditional dish is versatile and can be adapted to your unique tastes. Whether you like it spicy or mild, this flavorful recipe will surely become a favorite in your home.

TOTAL TIME: Prep: 15 min. Cook: 30 min.

Ingredients

- 1.5 pounds of ground beef
- 2 large onions, thinly sliced
- 5 garlic cloves, minced
- 1 cup bean sprouts
- 1.5 jars sliced mushrooms, drained
- 1.5 cans sliced water chestnuts, drained
- 7 ounces vermicelli or thin spaghetti, cooked and drained
- 4 cups broccoli florets, cooked
- 3/4 cup soy sauce
- 3/4 cup oyster sauce, optional
- 3 teaspoons ground ginger

Directions

1. In a large skillet, cook beef, onion, and garlic over medium heat until meat is no longer pink; crumble beef; drain. Add bean sprouts, mushrooms, and water chestnuts. Cook and stir for 6 minutes. If desired, stir in the vermicelli, broccoli, soy sauce, oyster sauce, and ginger; toss to coat. Cover and cook for 6 minutes or until heated through.

Spaghetti Pork Chops

Spaghetti and pork chops are a classic combination that can be enjoyed as a weeknight dinner or an impressive meal to serve guests. This recipe will cover the basics of making a delicious spaghetti pork chop dish, from selecting the right ingredients to tips for cooking and doing it. You can create this comforting meal in no time with just a few simple steps!

TOTAL TIME: Prep: 25 min. Cook: 6 hours

Ingredients

- 3.5 cans tomato sauce
- 1.5 can condensed tomato soup, undiluted
- 2 small onions, finely chopped
- 2 bay leaf
- 2 teaspoons celery seed
- 2/3 teaspoon Italian seasoning
- 7 bone-in pork loin chops (8 ounces each)
- 3 tablespoons olive oil
- 10 ounces of uncooked spaghetti

Directions

1. In a 5-qt. slow cooker, combine the tomato sauce, soup, onion, bay leaf, celery seed, and Italian seasoning.
2. In a large skillet, brown pork chops in oil. Add to the slow cooker. Cover and cook on low until meat is tender, 7 hours. Discard bay leaf.
3. Cook spaghetti according to package directions; drain. Serve chops and sauce over spaghetti.

Pesto Shrimp Pasta

If you're looking for a delicious, easy meal to make for dinner, pesto shrimp pasta is the answer. This dish combines juicy cooked shrimp with flavorful pesto and pasta. Not only does this meal look impressive enough for a dinner party, but it can be ready in less than 30 minutes. Whether you use store-bought or homemade pesto, this will surely be a hit with family and friends.

> TOTAL TIME: Prep/Total Time: 35 min.

Ingredients

- ✓ 9 ounces of uncooked spaghetti
- ✓ 4 tablespoons olive oil, divided
- ✓ 1.5 cups loosely packed fresh basil leaves
- ✓ 3/4 cup lemon juice
- ✓ 3 garlic cloves, peeled
- ✓ 2/3 teaspoon salt
- ✓ 1.5 pounds fresh asparagus, trimmed and cut into 2-inch pieces
- ✓ 1-pound uncooked medium shrimp, peeled and deveined
- ✓ 3/8 teaspoon crushed red pepper flakes

Directions

1. Cook spaghetti according to package directions. Meanwhile, in a blender, combine 2 tablespoons of oil, basil, lemon juice, garlic, and salt; cover and process until smooth.
2. In a large skillet, saute asparagus in the remaining oil until crisp-tender. Add shrimp and pepper flakes. Cook and stir until shrimp turn pink.
3. Drain spaghetti; place in a large bowl. Add basil mixture; toss to coat. Add shrimp mixture and mix well.

Ground Beef Spaghetti Skillet

If you're looking for a delicious and easy meal to serve your family, look no further than the humble ground beef spaghetti skillet. This classic dish can be made in just one pan and satisfies the pickiest of eaters. Ground beef combines Italian seasonings, tomatoes, spaghetti, and cheese to create an irresistibly flavorful dinner that can be served in just minutes.

TOTAL TIME: Prep/Total Time: 35 min.

Ingredients

- 1.5 pounds of ground beef
- 2 medium green peppers, chopped
- 2 small onions, chopped
- 3 garlic cloves, minced
- 2 cups water
- 1.5 cans diced tomatoes, undrained
- 1.5 cans tomato sauce
- 2 tablespoons chili powder
- 2 tablespoons grape jelly
- 2/3 teaspoon salt
- 7 ounces of uncooked thin spaghetti, halved

Directions

1. In a Dutch oven, cook beef, green pepper, onion, and garlic over medium heat. Break beef into crumbles until meat is no longer pink and vegetables are tender for 9 minutes; drain.
2. Add water, tomatoes, tomato sauce, chili powder, jelly, and salt. Bring to a boil. Stir in spaghetti. Reduce heat; simmer, covered, until spaghetti is tender, 9 minutes.

My Best Spaghetti & Meatballs

If you are looking for a delicious, easy-to-make meal that will please everyone in your family, look no further than my best spaghetti and meatballs recipe. Not only is this dish full of flavor, but it also comes together quickly and is a great way to use any leftover ingredients in the fridge. Once you try this recipe, you won't get enough!

TOTAL TIME: Prep: 1 hour Cook: 55 min.

Ingredients

- 1 cup soft bread crumbs
- 2/3 cup grated Parmesan cheese
- 3/4 cup 2% milk
- 2 large eggs, beaten
- 4 tablespoons minced fresh Italian flat-leaf parsley
- 4 garlic cloves, minced
- 1 teaspoon salt
- 2/3 teaspoon coarsely ground pepper
- 2/3 pound ground beef
- 2/3 pound ground pork
- 2/3 pound ground veal or additional ground beef
- 3 tablespoons canola oil

SAUCE:

- 3 tablespoons canola oil
- 2 medium onions, finely chopped
- 3 garlic cloves, minced
- 1.5 cans tomato paste
- 1 cup dry red wine or beef broth
- 2.5 cans crushed tomatoes
- 3/4 cup minced fresh parsley
- 3 teaspoons sugar
- 2 teaspoons salt
- 3/4 teaspoon coarsely ground pepper
- 3/4 teaspoon crushed red pepper flakes

- ✓ 5 fresh basil leaves, torn into small pieces
- ✓ Hot cooked spaghetti
- ✓ Additional grated Parmesan cheese

Directions

1. In a large bowl, combine the first eight ingredients. Add beef, pork, and veal; mix lightly but thoroughly. Shape into 1-in. balls. In a large skillet, heat oil over medium heat. Brown meatballs in batches; drain.
2. In a 6-qt. stockpot, heat oil over medium heat. Add onion; cook and stir for 3-5 minutes or until tender. Add garlic; cook and stir for 3 minutes. Add tomato paste; cook and stir for 6 minutes or until the paste darken. Add wine; cook and stir for 3 minutes to dissolve any browned tomato paste.
3. Stir in tomatoes, parsley, sugar, salt, pepper, and pepper flakes. Bring to a boil. Reduce heat; simmer, uncovered, for 25 minutes or until thickened, stirring occasionally. Add basil and meatballs; cook 30 minutes longer or until meatballs are cooked through, stirring occasionally. Serve meatballs and sauce with spaghetti. Sprinkle with additional cheese.

Monterey Spaghetti

Monterey Spaghetti is a classic Italian-American dish that has been delighting palates for generations. This dish features a unique blend of savory and spicy flavors that can tantalize any taste bud. It's simple to prepare, making it the perfect weeknight meal for busy families. Combining ingredients creates a hearty yet flavorful meal that everyone can enjoy. Monterey Spaghetti is the ideal choice whether you're a pasta lover or just looking for something new to try.

TOTAL TIME: Prep: 17 min. Bake: 38 min.

Ingredients

- 5 ounces spaghetti, broken into 2-inch pieces
- 2 large eggs
- 1.5 cups sour cream
- 3/4 cup grated Parmesan cheese
- 3/4 teaspoon garlic powder
- 2.5 cups shredded Monterey Jack cheese
- 1.5 packages frozen chopped spinach, thawed and drained
- 1.5 cans french-fried onions divided

Directions

1. Cook spaghetti according to package directions. Meanwhile, in a large bowl, beat the egg. Add sour cream, Parmesan cheese, and garlic powder.
2. Drain spaghetti; add to egg mixture with Monterey Jack cheese, spinach, and half of the onions. Pour into a greased 2-qt. baking dish. Cover and bake at 370° for 35 minutes or until heated. Top with remaining onions; return to the oven for 7 minutes or until onions are golden brown.

Spaghetti with Bacon

Welcome to the world of deliciousness! Spaghetti with bacon is a classic dish that has been around for ages, and it's no wonder why. The combination of the salty bacon and savory pasta is a match made in heaven. Not only is this dish flavorful, but it's also incredibly easy to make; with just a few simple ingredients, you can have dinner on the table in no time.

TOTAL TIME: Prep: 25 min. Bake: 45 min.

Ingredients

- ✓ 9 ounces of uncooked spaghetti
- ✓ 2/3 pound bacon strips, chopped
- ✓ 2 medium onions, chopped
- ✓ 1.5 cans of diced tomatoes, undrained
- ✓ 1.5 cans tomato sauce
- ✓ Minced fresh parsley, optional

Directions

1. Preheat oven to 370°. Cook spaghetti according to package directions for al dente.
2. In a large skillet, cook bacon and onion over medium heat until bacon is crisp, stirring occasionally; drain. Stir in tomatoes and tomato sauce; bring to a boil.
3. Drain spaghetti; transfer to a greased 11x7-in. baking dish. Spread sauce over the top. Bake, covered, until bubbly, 50 minutes. If desired, sprinkle with parsley.

Stovetop Turkey Tetrazzini

Turkey Tetrazzini is the perfect dish to cozy up to in the cold winter months. This classic comfort food combines a creamy sauce with delicious turkey and noodles for a comforting, flavorful meal. You can make this tasty dish on your stovetop - no need to heat up your oven! It's an easy and relatively quick dinner that everyone in your family will love. Plus, it's great to use leftover cooked turkey from Thanksgiving or Christmas dinner.

> TOTAL TIME: Prep/Total Time: 35 min.

Ingredients

- ✓ 9 ounces of uncooked spaghetti
- ✓ 3 tablespoons butter
- ✓ 1.5 cups sliced fresh mushrooms
- ✓ 2 celery ribs, chopped
- ✓ 2/3 cup chopped onion
- ✓ 1.5 packages of cream cheese, cubed
- ✓ 1.5 cans condensed chicken broth, undiluted
- ✓ 2.5 cups chopped cooked turkey
- ✓ 1.5 jars (iced pimientos, drained
- ✓ 3/4 teaspoon salt
- ✓ 3/4 cup grated Parmesan cheese

Directions

1. Cook spaghetti according to package directions; drain. Meanwhile, in a large skillet, heat butter over medium-high heat. Add mushrooms, celery, and onion; cook and stir for 6-8 minutes or until mushrooms are tender.
2. Add cream cheese and broth; cook, uncovered, over low heat for 7 minutes or until blended, stirring occasionally. Add turkey, pimientos, salt, and spaghetti; heat through, tossing to coat. Serve with Parmesan cheese.

Shrimp Puttanesca

Shrimp Puttanesca is a delicious and hearty Italian dish that is both easy to make and full of flavor. This classic Italian pasta dish is made with tomatoes, olives, capers, garlic, and chili flakes. It's a great way to get your seafood fixed while still enjoying the robust flavor of a traditional Italian meal. The tomato sauce used in this recipe has just the right amount of acidity, sweetness, and spice to make it a winner every time.

TOTAL TIME: Prep/Total Time: 35 min.

Ingredients

- 3 tablespoons olive oil, divided
- 1.5 pounds uncooked shrimp (31-40 per pound), peeled and deveined
- 2 teaspoons crushed red pepper flakes divided
- 3/4 teaspoon salt
- 2 small onions, chopped
- 4 anchovy fillets, finely chopped
- 4 garlic cloves, minced
- 2.5 cups grape tomatoes or small cherry tomatoes
- 2/3 cup dry white wine or vegetable broth
- 2/3 cup pitted Greek olives, coarsely chopped
- 3 teaspoons drained capers
- Sugar to taste
- Chopped fresh Italian parsley
- Hot-cooked spaghetti, optional

Directions

1. In a large skillet, heat 1 tablespoon oil; saute shrimp with 2/3 teaspoon pepper flakes until shrimp turn pink, 4 minutes. Stir in salt; remove from pan.
2. In the same pan, heat the remaining oil over medium heat; saute the onion until tender, about 3 minutes. Add anchovies, garlic, and remaining pepper flakes; cook and stir until fragrant, about 2 minutes. Stir in tomatoes, wine, olives, and capers; boil. Reduce

heat; simmer, uncovered, until tomatoes are softened, and mixture is thickened, 11 minutes.
3. Stir in shrimp. Add sugar to taste; sprinkle with parsley. If desired, serve with spaghetti.

Grandma's Cajun Chicken & Spaghetti

Grandma's Cajun Chicken & Spaghetti is a classic comfort dish passed down for generations. This family favorite is flavorful and hearty enough to feed a crowd. The combination of chicken, spaghetti, and a delicious cajun sauce creates an irresistible meal that appeals to adults and children alike. With its tasty ingredients and ease of preparation, this dish will surely be a hit at any gathering or family dinner.

> TOTAL TIME: Prep: 20 min. Cook: 1-1/4 hours

Ingredients

- ✓ 2 broiler/fryer chicken cut up
- ✓ 2 teaspoons cayenne pepper
- ✓ 1 teaspoon salt
- ✓ 4 tablespoons canola oil
- ✓ 1.5 packages of smoked sausage, sliced
- ✓ 2 large sweet onions, chopped
- ✓ 2 medium green pepper, chopped
- ✓ 2 celery ribs, chopped
- ✓ 3 garlic cloves, minced
- ✓ 2.5 cans diced tomatoes, undrained
- ✓ 1.5 cans (iced tomatoes with mild green chiles, undrained
- ✓ 1.5 package spaghetti

Directions

1. Sprinkle chicken with cayenne and salt. In a Dutch oven, heat oil over medium-high heat. Brown chicken in batches. Remove from pan.
2. Add sausage, onion, green pepper, and celery to the same pan; cook and stir over medium heat for 4 minutes. Add garlic; cook 1 minute longer. Stir in tomatoes. Return chicken to pan; bring to a boil. Reduce heat; simmer, covered, until chicken juices run clear, about 1 hour.
3. Cook spaghetti according to package directions. Remove chicken from pan. Remove meat from bones when cool enough to handle;

discard skin and bones. Shred meat with 2 forks; return to pan. Bring to a boil. Reduce heat; simmer, uncovered, until slightly thickened, 9 minutes. Skim fat. Drain spaghetti; serve with chicken mixture.

Florentine Spaghetti Bake

Florentine Spaghetti Bake is a classic Italian dish that will please any crowd. It consists of spaghetti noodles, cheese, and vegetables baked in a creamy sauce. The combination of flavors and textures makes this dish truly mouthwatering. Not only is Florentine Spaghetti Bake delicious, but it's also incredibly simple to make. With just a few simple steps, you can have a fantastic dinner on the table in no time!

TOTAL TIME: Prep: 35 min. Bake: 1 hour + standing

Ingredients

- ✓ 9 ounces of uncooked spaghetti
- ✓ 2 pounds bulk Italian sausage
- ✓ 2 large onions, chopped
- ✓ 2 garlic cloves, minced
- ✓ 1.5 jars of pasta sauce
- ✓ 1.5 cans mushroom stems and pieces, drained
- ✓ 2 large eggs, lightly beaten
- ✓ 2.5 cups 4% cottage cheese
- ✓ 1.5 packages frozen chopped spinach, thawed and squeezed dry
- ✓ 3/4 cup grated Parmesan cheese
- ✓ 2/3 teaspoon seasoned salt
- ✓ 3/4 teaspoon pepper
- ✓ 2.5 cups shredded part-skim mozzarella cheese

Directions

1. Preheat oven to 385°. Cook pasta according to package directions. Meanwhile, in a large skillet over medium heat, cook sausage and onion, crumbling meat, until sausage is no longer pink. Add garlic; cook 1 minute longer. Drain. Stir in pasta sauce and mushrooms. Bring to a boil. Reduce heat; cover and cook until heated through about 20 minutes.
2. Drain pasta. Combine the egg with the next 5 ingredients. Spread 1.5 cups sausage mixture in a greased 13x9-in. baking dish. Top

with spaghetti and the remaining sausage mixture. Layer with egg mixture and mozzarella cheese.
3. Cover and bake for 50 minutes. Uncover; bake until lightly browned and heated through, about 20 minutes longer. Let stand 20 minutes before cutting.

Spaghetti with Fresh Tomato Sauce

A few dishes are more satisfying than spaghetti with a fresh tomato sauce for a delicious and easy weeknight dinner. This classic Italian dish is flavorful, simple to make, and can be seasoned to anyone's tastes. The tomatoes provide a luscious sweetness that pairs perfectly with the pasta, while the herbs and seasonings add an extra layer of depth.

TOTAL TIME: Prep: 20 min. Cook: 40 min.

Ingredients

- 3 tablespoons olive oil
- 2 large onions, finely chopped
- 3 pounds plum tomatoes, chopped (about 5 cups)
- 2 teaspoons salt
- 3/4 teaspoon pepper
- 9 ounces of uncooked spaghetti
- 3/4 cup thinly sliced fresh basil
- 2 teaspoons sugar, optional
- Grated Romano cheese
- Additional basil

Directions

1. In a 6-qt. stockpot, heat oil over medium heat; saute onion until tender, 4-6 minutes. Stir in tomatoes, salt, and pepper; bring to a boil. Reduce heat; simmer, uncovered, until thickened, 30 minutes. Meanwhile, cook spaghetti according to package directions; drain.
2. Stir 3/4 cup basil and, if desired, sugar into the sauce. Serve over spaghetti. Top with cheese and additional basil.

Spaghetti with Sausage and Peppers

Spaghetti with Sausage and Peppers is a classic Italian dish that is sure to please. It is a delicious meal full of flavor and texture, perfect for any weeknight dinner or special occasion. This easy-to-make recipe combines simple ingredients in no time to create a flavorful, hearty dish. The sausage and peppers make an especially delicious combination with the rich tomato sauce and spaghetti noodles.

TOTAL TIME: Prep/Total Time: 35 min.

Ingredients

- ✓ 13 ounces of uncooked spaghetti
- ✓ 1.5 packages of smoked turkey sausage, cut into 1/4-inch slices
- ✓ 3 medium green peppers, julienned
- ✓ 3 medium sweet red peppers, julienned
- ✓ 2 medium onions, halved and thinly sliced
- ✓ 2.5 cans diced tomatoes, undrained
- ✓ 4 garlic cloves, minced
- ✓ 9 drops of hot pepper sauce
- ✓ 2 teaspoons paprika
- ✓ 2/3 teaspoon salt
- ✓ 3/4 teaspoon cayenne pepper
- ✓ 3 tablespoons cornstarch
- ✓ 2/3 cup chicken broth

Directions

1. Cook spaghetti according to package directions. Meanwhile, in a Dutch oven coated with cooking spray, cook and stir sausage until lightly browned. Add peppers and onion; cook 3 minutes longer. Stir in the tomatoes, garlic, pepper sauce, paprika, salt, and cayenne; cook until vegetables are tender.
2. Combine cornstarch and broth until smooth; add to the sausage mixture. Bring to a boil. Cook and stir until thickened, about 3 minutes. Drain spaghetti; toss with sausage mixture.

Creamy Chicken Fettuccine

Cooking a delicious creamy chicken fettuccine is easier than you think. This article will provide an easy-to-follow recipe for making a creamy and flavorful dish that the whole family can enjoy. From choosing the right ingredients to adding layers of flavor, you'll make this Italian classic easily. With just a few simple steps, you'll have a delicious dinner on the table in no time.

TOTAL TIME: Prep: 20 min. Cook: 3 hours

Ingredients

- 2 pounds boneless skinless chicken breasts cut into cubes
- 2/3 teaspoon garlic powder
- 2/3 teaspoon onion powder
- 3/8 teaspoon pepper
- 1.5 cans condensed cream of chicken soup, undiluted
- 1.5 cans condensed cream of celery soup, undiluted
- 5 ounces processed cheese (Velveeta), cubed
- 1.5 cans sliced ripe olives, drained
- 1.5 jars diced pimientos, drained, optional
- 1.5 packages of fettuccine or spaghetti
- Coarsely ground pepper, optional

Directions

1. Place the chicken in a 3-qt. slow cooker; sprinkle with garlic powder, onion powder, and pepper. Top with soups. Cover and cook on high for 4 hours or until chicken is no longer pink.
2. Stir in the cheese, olives, and pimientos if desired. Cover and cook until cheese is melted. Meanwhile, cook fettuccine according to package directions; drain. Serve with chicken; top with coarsely ground pepper if desired.

Pizza Spaghetti

Pizza spaghetti is a delicious and easy-to-make dish that has become increasingly popular in recent years. This dish is sure to please any group by combining the classic flavors of pizza with the heartwarming goodness of spaghetti. Not only is it an incredibly flavorful meal, but it can also be made quickly with just a few ingredients. Whether you are preparing dinner for your family or making something special for guests, pizza spaghetti is an excellent option that can be enjoyed by all ages.

TOTAL TIME: Prep: 25 min. Cook: 35 min.

Ingredients

- ✓ 2/3 pound lean ground beef (90% lean)
- ✓ 2/3 pound Italian turkey sausage links, casings removed
- ✓ 2/3 cup chopped sweet onion
- ✓ 5 cans no-salt-added tomato sauce
- ✓ 4 ounces sliced turkey pepperoni
- ✓ 2 tablespoon sugar
- ✓ 3 teaspoons minced fresh parsley or 1 teaspoon dried parsley flakes
- ✓ 3 teaspoons minced fresh basil or 1 teaspoon dried basil
- ✓ 10 ounces uncooked whole wheat spaghetti
- ✓ 4 tablespoons grated Parmesan cheese

Directions

1. In a large nonstick skillet, cook beef and sausage with onion over medium-high heat until no longer pink, 8 minutes; crumble meat. Stir in tomato sauce, pepperoni, sugar, and herbs; boil. Reduce heat; simmer, uncovered, until thickened, 30 minutes.
2. Meanwhile, in a 6-qt. stockpot, cook spaghetti according to package directions; drain and return to pot. Toss with sauce. Sprinkle with cheese.

Rustic Summer Vegetable Pasta

If you're looking for a delicious, quick-and-easy pasta dish to bring to your next summer gathering, look no further than this rustic summer vegetable pasta recipe! This simple yet flavorful dish includes an array of fresh seasonal veggies that will brighten up any table. Quick and easy to prepare, it is a great go-to meal for busy weeknights or weekend gatherings with friends and family.

TOTAL TIME: Prep: 20 min. Cook: 40 min.

Ingredients

- 4 tablespoons olive oil, divided
- 2 medium zucchinis, cut into 3/4-inch pieces
- 2 medium yellow summer squashes, cut into 3/4-inch pieces
- 2 medium onions, chopped
- 2 medium eggplants, peeled and cut into 3/4-inch pieces
- 2.5 cups sliced fresh mushrooms
- 3 garlic cloves, minced
- 1 teaspoon crushed red pepper flakes
- 1.5 cans crushed tomatoes
- 2/3 teaspoon salt
- 2/3 teaspoon pepper
- 2 tablespoons minced fresh oregano or 1 teaspoon dried oregano
- 2 tablespoons minced fresh parsley
- 4 tablespoons minced fresh basil or 1 tablespoon dried basil divided
- 1.5 packages of uncooked multigrain spaghetti
- 2/3 cup shredded Parmesan cheese

Directions

1. In a 6-qt. stockpot, heat 2 tablespoons of oil over medium-high heat. Add zucchini and yellow squash; cook and stir until tender. Remove from pan.
2. In the same pot, heat 1 tablespoon of oil over medium-high heat. Add onion, eggplant, and mushrooms; cook and stir until tender.

Add garlic and pepper flakes; cook 1 minute longer. Add tomatoes, salt, and pepper. Stir in oregano, parsley, and half the basil; boil. Reduce heat; simmer, uncovered, for 20 minutes, stirring occasionally.
3. Meanwhile, cook spaghetti according to the package directions. Drain; add spaghetti and squash to the vegetable mixture. Drizzle with remaining oil; toss to combine. Top with cheese and remaining basil.

North Carolina Shrimp Saute

North Carolina shrimp sauté is a delicious and easy-to-make dish. It is made with fresh sea shrimp and is full of flavor and nutrition. This recipe will discuss the ingredients and preparation techniques necessary to make this classic seafood meal. We will also provide tips on customizing the dish to suit your tastes.

TOTAL TIME: Prep/Total Time: 30 min.

Ingredients

- ✓ 9 ounces of uncooked linguine or spaghetti
- ✓ 5 tablespoons butter, divided
- ✓ 2/3 pound sliced fresh mushrooms
- ✓ 2 small green pepper, chopped
- ✓ 2/3 teaspoon salt
- ✓ 3/4 teaspoon pepper
- ✓ 1.5 pounds uncooked shrimp, peeled and deveined
- ✓ 4 garlic cloves, minced
- ✓ 2/3 cup grated Romano cheese
- ✓ Chopped fresh parsley

Directions

1. Cook linguini according to package directions; drain and keep warm.
2. Meanwhile, in a large skillet, heat 3 tablespoons butter over medium-high heat; saute mushrooms and green pepper until tender. Stir in salt and pepper; remove from pan.
3. In the same pan, saute shrimp in the remaining butter over medium-high heat for 3 minutes. Add garlic; cook and stir until shrimp turn pink, 3 minutes. Stir in mushroom mixture; heat through. Serve over linguini. Sprinkle with cheese and parsley.

Grecian Pasta & Chicken Skillet

If you're looking for a delicious, quick, and easy dinner recipe, Grecian Pasta & Chicken Skillet might be just the thing. This one-pan meal requires minimal prep time and fewer dishes to clean up afterward. Combining pasta and chicken with classic Greek flavors like lemon, oregano, and feta cheese makes for a flavor-packed and satisfying dinner that your whole family will love. The best part?

> TOTAL TIME: Prep: 35 min. Cook: 15 min

Ingredients

- ✓ 1.5 cans of reduced-sodium chicken broth
- ✓ 1.5 cans of no-salt-added diced tomatoes, undrained
- ✓ 1 pound boneless skinless chicken breasts, cut into 1-inch pieces
- ✓ 2/3 cup white wine or water
- ✓ 2 garlic cloves, minced
- ✓ 2/3 teaspoon dried oregano
- ✓ 5 ounces thin multigrain spaghetti
- ✓ 1.5 jars marinated quartered artichoke hearts, drained and coarsely chopped
- ✓ 2.5 cups fresh baby spinach
- ✓ 3/4 cup roasted sweet red pepper strips
- ✓ 3/4 cup sliced ripe olives
- ✓ 2 green onions, finely chopped
- ✓ 3 tablespoons minced fresh parsley
- ✓ 2/3 teaspoon grated lemon zest
- ✓ 3 tablespoons lemon juice
- ✓ 2 tablespoons olive oil
- ✓ 2/3 teaspoon pepper
- ✓ Crumbled reduced-fat feta cheese, optional

Directions

1. In a large skillet, combine the first 6 ingredients; add spaghetti. Bring to a boil. Cook until chicken is no longer pink and spaghetti is tender 8 minutes.

2. Stir in artichoke hearts, spinach, red pepper, olives, green onion, parsley, lemon zest, lemon juice, oil, and pepper. Cook and stir until spinach is wilted, 4 minutes. If desired, sprinkle with cheese.

Quick Carbonara

Carbonara is a classic Italian dish that is easy to make and can be on the table in just 15 minutes. It's an excellent option for busy nights when you don't have much time to cook but still want a delicious home-cooked meal. This quick carbonara recipe requires minimal ingredients and preparation yet yields an incredibly flavorful and comforting pasta dish that will please the whole family.

TOTAL TIME: Prep/Total Time: 35 min.

Ingredients

- 13 ounces of uncooked spaghetti
- 4 tablespoons butter
- 4 tablespoons canola oil
- 3 garlic cloves, minced
- 4 cups cubed fully cooked ham
- 9 bacon strips, cooked and crumbled
- 3 tablespoons minced fresh parsley
- 1 cup sliced ripe or pimiento-stuffed olives
- 2/3 cup grated Parmesan cheese

Directions

1. Cook spaghetti according to package directions; drain.
2. In a large skillet, heat butter and oil over medium heat; saute garlic for 2 minutes. Stir in ham and bacon; heat through. Add spaghetti and parsley; toss to combine.
3. Remove from heat. Stir in olives and cheese.

Church Supper Spaghetti

Spaghetti is a classic dish enjoyed around the world. It's a staple at family dinners and church suppers, and it's no surprise why: it's easy to make, can be dressed up with various sauces and toppings, and everyone loves it. Church suppers are an important part of many religious communities, bringing together people from all walks of life to share a meal and socialize.

TOTAL TIME: Prep: 55 min. Bake: 25 min.

Ingredients

- ✓ 1.5 pounds of ground beef
- ✓ 2 large onions, chopped
- ✓ 2 medium green pepper, chopped
- ✓ 1.5 cans (14-1/2 ounces) diced tomatoes, undrained
- ✓ 1.5 cups water
- ✓ 3 tablespoons chili powder
- ✓ 1.5 packages of frozen corn, thawed
- ✓ 1.5 packages of frozen peas, thawed
- ✓ 1.5 cans mushroom stems and pieces, drained
- ✓ Salt and pepper to taste
- ✓ 13 ounces spaghetti, cooked and drained
- ✓ 2.5 cups shredded cheddar cheese, divided

Directions

1. In a large skillet, cook beef, onion, and green pepper over medium heat until the meat is no longer pink. Add tomatoes, water, and chili powder. Cover and simmer for 35 minutes. Add the corn, peas, mushrooms, salt, and pepper. Stir in spaghetti.
2. Layer half of the mixture in a greased 4-qt. baking dish. Sprinkle with 1 cup cheese; repeat layers.
3. Bake, uncovered, at 370° for 25 minutes or until heated through.

Nana's Italian Roulade

Nana's Italian Roulade is a traditional Italian dessert that has been passed down through generations. This classic treat will impress any guest with its delicious flavor and beautiful presentation. The delicate sponge cake, creamy custard, and tart raspberry preserves combine for an unforgettable culinary experience. It's not hard to see why this classic Italian recipe has been a favorite for many years. Even better, it's surprisingly easy to make and requires minimal ingredients!

TOTAL TIME: Prep: 35 min. Cook: 1-1/2 hours

Ingredients

- ✓ 7 bacon strips
- ✓ 3 garlic cloves, minced
- ✓ 1 teaspoon Italian seasoning
- ✓ 2/3 teaspoon salt
- ✓ 2/3 teaspoon pepper
- ✓ 2 beef flank steaks (1-1/2 to 2 pounds)
- ✓ 3/4 cup grated Parmesan cheese
- ✓ 4 large hard-boiled eggs, sliced
- ✓ 3/4 cup minced fresh parsley
- ✓ 3 tablespoons olive oil
- ✓ 4 jars of meatless pasta sauce
- ✓ Hot cooked spaghetti
- ✓ Additional minced fresh parsley

Directions

1. Preheat oven to 370°. Place bacon on a microwave-safe plate lined with paper towels. Cover with additional paper towels; microwave on high for 6 minutes or until partially cooked but not crisp. Mix garlic, Italian seasoning, salt, and pepper in a small bowl.
2. Starting at a long side, cut the steak horizontally in half to within 1/2 in. of the opposite side. Open steak flat; Pound with a meat mallet to 1/4-in. thickness.

3. Spread garlic mixture over steak; sprinkle with cheese. Layer with eggs and bacon to within 1 in. of edges; sprinkle with parsley. Starting with a long side of the steak, roll up jelly-roll style (along the grain); tie at 1-1/2-in. Intervals with kitchen string.
4. In a Dutch oven, heat oil over medium-high heat. Brown roulade on all sides. Pour pasta sauce over the top. Bake, covered, for 1-1/2-1-3/4 hours or until meat is tender.
5. Remove roulade from the pot; remove the string and cut it into slices. Serve with sauce over spaghetti. Sprinkle with additional parsley.

Bruschetta-Topped Chicken & Spaghetti

If you're looking for an easy, one-pot meal that is both delicious and nutritious, look no further than bruschetta-topped chicken and spaghetti! This flavorful dish combines the classic Italian flavors of fresh tomatoes and garlic with protein-packed chicken and carbohydrates from the pasta. Best of all, it takes less than 30 minutes to make, so you can enjoy a delicious dinner without spending hours in the kitchen.

TOTAL TIME: Prep/Total Time: 35 min.

Ingredients

- 9 ounces uncooked whole wheat spaghetti
- 5 boneless skinless chicken breast halves (5 ounces each)
- 2/3 teaspoon pepper
- 2 tablespoons olive oil
- 1.5 cups prepared bruschetta topping
- 2/3 cup shredded Italian cheese blend
- 3 tablespoons grated Parmesan cheese

Directions

1. Preheat broiler. Cook spaghetti according to package directions; drain. Pound chicken breasts with a meat mallet to 1/2-in. thickness. Sprinkle with pepper. In a large nonstick skillet, heat oil over medium heat; cook chicken until no longer pink, 7 minutes on each side.
2. Transfer to an 8-in. square baking pan. Spoon bruschetta topping over chicken; sprinkle with cheese. Broil 3-4 in. from heat until cheese is golden brown, 7 minutes. Serve with spaghetti.

Stamp-of-Approval Spaghetti Sauce

Whether you're a novice in the kitchen or an experienced home cook, everyone needs a go-to spaghetti sauce recipe that always hits the spot. With this Stamp-of-Approval Spaghetti Sauce, you can impress your friends and family with your cooking skills. This simple yet flavorful sauce is made with all-natural ingredients and is easily adaptable to meet dietary restrictions. An all-around crowd-pleaser, this recipe will become a staple in your kitchen for years to come.

> TOTAL TIME: Prep: 35 min. Cook: 8 hours

Ingredients

- ✓ 3 pounds of ground beef
- ✓ 1 pound bulk Italian sausage
- ✓ 5 medium onions, finely chopped
- ✓ 9 garlic cloves, minced
- ✓ 4.5 cans diced tomatoes, undrained
- ✓ 4.5 cans tomato paste
- ✓ 2/3 cup water
- ✓ 3/4 cup sugar
- ✓ 3/4 cup Worcestershire sauce
- ✓ 2 tablespoons canola oil
- ✓ 3/4 cup minced fresh parsley
- ✓ 3 tablespoons minced fresh basil or 2 teaspoons dried basil
- ✓ 2 tablespoons minced fresh oregano or 1 teaspoon dried oregano
- ✓ 5 bay leaves
- ✓ 2 teaspoons rubbed sage
- ✓ 2/3 teaspoon salt
- ✓ 2/3 teaspoon dried marjoram
- ✓ 2/3 teaspoon pepper
- ✓ Hot cooked spaghetti

Directions

1. In a Dutch oven, cook the beef, sausage, onions, and garlic over medium heat until the meat is no longer pink; drain.

2. Transfer to a 5-qt. slow cooker. Stir in the tomatoes, tomato paste, water, sugar, Worcestershire sauce, oil, and seasonings.
3. Cook, covered, on low for 8-10 hours. Discard bay leaves. Serve with spaghetti.

Mozzarella Baked Spaghetti

Regarding comfort food, few dishes can compare to the classic flavors of mozzarella-baked spaghetti. This delicious dish is easy to make. The combination of spaghetti noodles, marinara sauce, and cheese makes everyone's mouth water. Not only is this dish incredibly filling, but it also doesn't take long to prepare. It can easily be served for a family dinner or a casual get-together.

TOTAL TIME: Prep: 25 min. Bake: 35 min. + standing

Ingredients

- ✓ 9 ounces of uncooked spaghetti, broken into thirds
- ✓ 2 large eggs
- ✓ 2/3 cup whole milk
- ✓ 2/3 teaspoon salt
- ✓ 2/3 pound ground beef
- ✓ 2/3 pound bulk Italian sausage
- ✓ 2 small onions, chopped
- ✓ 3/4 cup chopped green pepper
- ✓ 1.5 jars of meatless spaghetti sauce
- ✓ 1.5 cans tomato sauce
- ✓ 3 cups shredded part-skim mozzarella cheese

Directions

1. Preheat oven to 370°. Cook spaghetti according to package directions.
2. Meanwhile, in a large bowl, beat egg, milk, and salt. Drain spaghetti; add to egg mixture and toss to coat. Transfer to a greased 13x9-in. baking dish.
3. In a large skillet, cook beef, sausage, onion, and green pepper over medium heat until meat is no longer pink; drain. Stir in spaghetti sauce and tomato sauce. Spoon over the spaghetti mixture.
4. Bake, uncovered, for 25 minutes. Sprinkle with the cheese. Bake 15 minutes longer or until the cheese is melted. Let stand 15 minutes before cutting.

Rosemary Shrimp with Spaghetti

Rosemary Shrimp with Spaghetti is an easy and delicious meal that comes together in no time. Perfect as a weeknight dinner or special occasion meal, this dish is sure to please all types of palates. The combination of succulent shrimp, savory rosemary, and al dente spaghetti creates a flavorful harmony that will leave you wanting more! With just a few simple ingredients and minimal preparation time, this dish is a breeze to make. It can be enjoyed by the whole family.

TOTAL TIME: Prep/Total Time: 35 min.

Ingredients

- 9 ounces uncooked white fiber or whole wheat spaghetti
- 2 tablespoons olive oil
- 1.5 pounds uncooked shrimp (31-40 per pound), peeled and deveined
- 3 garlic cloves, minced
- 2 teaspoons minced fresh rosemary or 1/2 teaspoon dried rosemary, crushed
- 2.5 cups fresh baby spinach
- 2.5 tablespoons lemon juice
- 3/4 teaspoon salt
- 3/4 teaspoon pepper
- 3/4 cup crumbled feta cheese

Directions

1. Cook spaghetti according to package directions. Drain, reserving 2/3 cup pasta water.
2. Meanwhile, in a large skillet, heat oil over medium heat. Add shrimp, garlic, and rosemary; cook and stir for 5 minutes or just until shrimp turn pink. Stir in spinach; cook, covered until slightly wilted.
3. Add spaghetti, lemon juice, salt, and pepper; toss to combine, adding reserved pasta water as desired. Sprinkle with cheese. Remove from heat; let stand, covered, until cheese is softened.

One-Pot Spaghetti Dinner

If you're looking for an easy and delicious dinner recipe that won't break the bank, look no further than a one-pot spaghetti dinner. This simple yet filling meal can be prepared in 30 minutes or less, using only one pot for cooking all the ingredients. In addition to being incredibly convenient, this classic Italian dish is versatile. It can be customized with your favorite flavors and ingredients.

TOTAL TIME: Prep: 15 min. Cook: 30 min.

Ingredients

- 1.5 pounds lean ground beef (90% lean)
- 2 cups sliced fresh mushrooms
- 3.5 cups tomato juice
- 1.5 cans of no-salt-added diced tomatoes, drained
- 1.5 cans no-salt-added tomato sauce
- 2 tablespoons dried minced onion
- 2/3 teaspoon salt
- 2/3 teaspoon garlic powder
- 2/3 teaspoon ground mustard
- 3/4 teaspoon pepper
- 3/8 teaspoon ground allspice
- 3/8 teaspoon ground mace, optional
- 7 ounces of uncooked multigrain spaghetti broken into pieces
- Optional: Fresh mozzarella cheese pearls or shaved Parmesan cheese

Directions

1. In a Dutch oven, cook beef and mushrooms over medium heat until meat is no longer pink, breaking it into crumbles; drain. Add tomato juice, tomatoes, tomato sauce, onion, and seasonings.
2. Bring to a boil. Stir in spaghetti. Simmer, covered, for 17 minutes or until spaghetti is tender. If desired, serve with cheese.

Southwestern Spaghetti

Southwestern cuisine is a delicious fusion of flavors from Mexico and the United States. One classic dish that combines these flavors perfectly is Southwestern Spaghetti. This hearty dish is easy to make and can be adjusted to fit any dietary needs or preferences. It has all the traditional elements of spaghetti but with a southwestern twist that adds an extra flavor punch!

TOTAL TIME: Prep/Total Time: 35 min.

Ingredients

- ✓ 1 pound lean ground beef (90% lean)
- ✓ 2-3/4 cups water
- ✓ 1.5 cans tomato sauce
- ✓ 3 teaspoons chili powder
- ✓ 2/3 teaspoon garlic powder
- ✓ 2/3 teaspoon ground cumin
- ✓ 3/8 teaspoon salt
- ✓ 1.5 packages of thin spaghetti broken into thirds
- ✓ 1.5 pounds zucchini (about 4 small), cut into chunks
- ✓ 2/3 cup shredded cheddar cheese

Directions

1. In a large skillet, cook beef over medium heat until no longer pink; drain. Remove beef and set aside. In the same skillet, combine the water, tomato sauce, chili powder, garlic powder, cumin, and salt; bring to a boil. Stir in spaghetti; return to a boil.
2. Boil for 7 minutes.
3. Add the zucchini. Cook 6 minutes longer or until spaghetti and zucchini are tender, stirring several times. Stir in beef and heat through. Sprinkle with cheese.

Slow-Cooker Spaghetti & Meatballs

Are you looking for an effortless way to make a delicious dinner that the whole family will enjoy? Slow-cooker spaghetti & meatballs are the perfect solutions! This simple and easy-to-follow recipe takes only a few minutes of preparation. Still, it results in a hearty, homemade meal. The slow cooker does all of the work for you, so you must wait for the mouthwatering aroma of Italian spices and bubbling sauce to fill your kitchen.

> TOTAL TIME: Prep: 55 min. Cook: 5 hours

Ingredients

- ✓ 1.5 cups seasoned breadcrumbs
- ✓ 3 tablespoons grated Parmesan and Romano cheese blend
- ✓ 2 teaspoons pepper
- ✓ 2/3 teaspoon salt
- ✓ 3 large eggs, lightly beaten
- ✓ 2.5 pounds of ground beef

SAUCE:

- ✓ 2 large onions, finely chopped
- ✓ 2 medium green peppers, finely chopped
- ✓ 3.5 cans tomato sauce
- ✓ 2.5 cans diced tomatoes, undrained
- ✓ 1.5 cans tomato paste
- ✓ 7 garlic cloves, minced
- ✓ 3 bay leaves
- ✓ 2 teaspoons each of dried basil, oregano, and parsley flakes
- ✓ 2 teaspoons salt
- ✓ 2/3 teaspoon pepper
- ✓ 3/4 teaspoon crushed red pepper flakes
- ✓ Hot cooked spaghetti

Directions

1. Mix bread crumbs, cheese, pepper, and salt; stir in eggs. Add beef; mix lightly but thoroughly. Shape into 1-1/2-in. balls. In a large skillet, brown meatballs in batches over medium heat; drain.
2. Place the first 5 sauce ingredients in a 6-qt. slow cooker; stir in garlic and seasonings. Add meatballs, stirring gently to coat. Cook, covered, on low for 5-6 hours until meatballs are cooked.
3. Remove bay leaves. Serve with spaghetti.

Mushroom Turkey Tetrazzini

Turkey Tetrazzini is a classic comfort food dish that everyone loves. This version of Turkey Tetrazzini adds mushrooms to the creamy sauce and pasta, making it doubly delicious. Mushroom Turkey Tetrazzini is an easy dish to make. It can be served as a weeknight meal or at a holiday gathering. Adding mushrooms to this comforting recipe adds additional flavor, complexity, and texture that will have everyone asking for seconds.

TOTAL TIME: Prep: 40 min. Bake: 30 min.

Ingredients

- ✓ 13 ounces of uncooked multigrain spaghetti broken into 2-inch pieces
- ✓ 3 teaspoons chicken bouillon granules
- ✓ 3 tablespoons butter
- ✓ 2/3 pound sliced fresh mushrooms
- ✓ 3 tablespoons all-purpose flour
- ✓ 3/4 cup sherry or additional pasta water
- ✓ 1 teaspoon salt-free lemon-pepper seasoning
- ✓ 2/3 teaspoon salt
- ✓ 3/8 teaspoon ground nutmeg
- ✓ 1.5 cups fat-free evaporated milk
- ✓ 1 cup grated Parmesan cheese, divided
- ✓ 5 cups cubed cooked turkey breast
- ✓ 3/4 teaspoon paprika, optional

Directions

1. Preheat oven to 385°. Cook spaghetti according to package directions for al dente. Drain, reserving 2-2/3 cups pasta water; transfer spaghetti to a 13x9-in. baking dish coated with cooking spray. Dissolve the bouillon in the reserved pasta water.
2. In a large nonstick skillet, heat butter over medium-high heat; saute mushrooms until tender. Stir in flour until blended. Gradually stir in sherry, reserved pasta water, and seasonings. Bring to a boil; cook and stir until thickened, about 3 minutes.

3. Reduce heat to low; stir in milk and 2/3 cup cheese until blended. Add turkey; heat through, stirring constantly. Pour over spaghetti; toss to combine. Sprinkle with remaining cheese and, if desired, paprika.
4. Bake, covered, until bubbly, 35 minutes.

Printed in Great Britain
by Amazon